To:
....
From:
....
Date:
....

D0952053

What's True About YOU

Life-Changing Reminders
of Who God Says You Are

HOLLEY GERTH

What's True About You: Life-Changing Reminders of Who God Says You Are
Copyright © 2019 by Holley Gerth
First Edition, March 2019

Published by:

DaySpring

P.O. Box 1010
Siloam Springs, AR 72761
dayspring.com

Designed by Heather Steck
Hand-lettered by Shelby Taylor
Printed in China
Prime: 89886
ISBN: 978-1-68408-614-6

Contents

Introduction

You are loved.

    You have a purpose.

    You're seen and valued.

    All of this, and more, is true about you today. Yet in the middle of our busy, broken world, the lies can get loud. Our hearts need a place to come back to where we can be reminded of what God says about us. This little book is a safe space where you can go anytime you're longing for strength, confidence, or encouragement. Set it on your nightstand. Keep it in your purse. Give it to the people you love.

    We'll never stop needing the reminders on these pages because other voices, and even our own feelings, will never stop trying to tell us who we really are or should be. Only we can decide God gets the final word over the lies. When we do, everything changes. We have more joy and less discouragement, more peace and less fear, more bravery and less insecurity. We can live more fully and love more deeply.

    We are God's creation. We are His beloved daughters. We have a hope and a future. What He says about us is true today and forever.

Holley

You Are *Loved* Anyway and Always

For I am persuaded that neither death nor life,
nor angels nor rulers, nor things present nor things
to come, nor powers, nor height nor depth, nor any other
created thing will be able to separate us from the love of
God that is in Christ Jesus our Lord.

ROMANS 8:38–39

*God, Your love is so far beyond our understanding.
Even if we can't fully comprehend it please help us to receive it,
embrace it, believe it with all our hearts. You are the One
who created us. You have a good plan for our lives.
You alone have determined our identity and destiny.
We are unconditionally, fully loved by You.
Amen.*

I stand at the kitchen stove and stir butter around a warm pan with a spoon. My thoughts feel mixed up too. I close my eyes and whisper the prayer I'm learning to cling to in these moments, "God, what do You want to say to my heart today?"

Usually a Scripture comes to mind. Sometimes I remember encouraging words from a wise friend. But this time a new phrase comes instantly: I love you anyway. Tears fill my eyes because it's exactly what I need to hear. My struggles make it seem as though God must be upset and far away. But He is still right there with me. And He is still for me.

When we battle depression, God loves us anyway.

When we fight anxiety, God loves us anyway.

When we mess up, God loves us anyway.

When we face doubts, God loves us anyway.

When we forget who we really are, God loves us anyway.

When we're weary, God loves us anyway.

Whatever we're struggling with today, God loves us anyway.

I carry my plate to the table and whisper, "God, help me truly believe I'm loved by You right now just as I am." My prayer is the same for you. May we be confident we're loved anyway. May we be certain we're loved always. Especially on the hard days.

You Have
Everything
You
Need

The LORD is my shepherd;
I have all that I need.

PSALM 23:1 NLT

God, You have promised to care for us.
We bring You the needs of our hearts,
the needs of our souls, the needs of our relationships,
the needs of our situations, and we trust
that You will meet them. You are our Provider,
our Comforter, the One who sustains us.
Amen.

There will never be a situation, conversation, or circumstance when God is not with us and working on our behalf. We will never walk into a room where He isn't already there. We will never receive news that He hasn't already heard. We will never face a challenge He hasn't already overcome.

Nothing surprises God because He knows the past, present, and future. He can't be derailed, disappointed, or deterred. He doesn't become discouraged. He doesn't grow weary. He doesn't give up, give in, or let go.

God has endless capacity, so He is the only One who can truly handle everything. *Nothing is too big for Him. And nothing is too small.* He can do it all. We can't be "too much" for Him and we can't be "not enough." Any limitation that causes us hesitation will not slow Him down.

He has promised to be our help. He has promised to be our hope. He has promised to get us through whatever happens. He has a plan for us and it's good. We can trust Him to complete His purposes for our lives because He loves us.

God is on our side. And He is by our side. With Him, we have everything we need for this day, tomorrow, and *forever.*

You Are
Extraordinary

Now we have this treasure in clay jars,
so that this extraordinary power
may be from God and not from us.

II CORINTHIANS 4:7

God, You are the One who makes us extraordinary.
It's not because of us or anything we do.
It's always and only because we are made in the image
of a star-scattering, water-walking, miracle-making God.
You empower us to be more than we ever could be
on our own. We ask You to do so today in ways
that are beyond what we can even imagine.

Amen.

It's hard to see anything remarkable about our existence when another morning comes and we're standing in the kitchen with a cup of coffee in our hands and a little bit of sleep left in our eyes. Sometimes in the middle of all our ordinary we can lose sight of what's eternally true.

So I'm whispering in your ear and to your heart that God living within you makes you extraordinary. Nothing can change that—not time or circumstances or even the mistakes you make. Even your weaknesses don't negate God's supreme workmanship. "Now we have this treasure in clay jars, so that this extraordinary power may be from God and not from us" (II Corinthians 4:7).

This phrase stands out to me most in that verse: *extraordinary power.* (Sometimes I don't even feel like I have the power to get out of bed on time.) But here's what's true: *there's nothing too difficult for us today because there's nothing too difficult for the God who lives in us.* And there's nothing ordinary about us or our lives because we have an extraordinary God inhabiting our hearts.

I praise YOU because You made me

in an amazing & wonderful way.

PSALM
139:14 NCV

You Are *Free*

For you were called to be free, brothers and sisters;
only don't use this freedom as an opportunity
for the flesh, but serve one another through love.

GALATIANS 5:13

God, You set us free from all that holds us back—
sin, shame, fear, hopelessness.
Then You invite us into a new way of living
that's filled with love, grace, and freedom.
Help us to embrace what's already ours because of You
and resist whatever threatens to confine and define
us in ways You never intended.
Amen.

We often picture God's will for our lives like a thin, definitive line. A tightrope we must walk carefully and with the utmost caution. One wrong step and we'll surely fall. And when we do, we'll mess up our future forever.

But when we come to know Jesus, our life is not a tightrope but a wide, open space of grace. We have so much room to breathe, to grow, to learn. God knows we are human. He knows we will take detours, face obstacles, and make mistakes. If He were committed to using only those of us who never stray, then no human would ever be part of His plan.

You are made to move in grace—not to be held in place by fear. You are guided by love and by a God who can redirect you as many times as needed. You only need to be willing to follow where He wants you to go. He will do the rest. Life is meant to be a glorious adventure, not a continual test in which one slipup means you fail.

You're not made to walk a tightrope.

You're made to dance.

And it's not about getting all the steps right.

Instead it's all about being close to your partner.

If We Could Have Coffee

You Have a *Place*

For we are His workmanship, created in
Christ Jesus for good works, which God
prepared ahead of time for us to do.

EPHESIANS 2:10

*God, You are continually revealing Yourself
in this generation and, mysteriously, You do so
through each of our lives—we all show parts
of who You are. Give us the courage to be ourselves
rather than believe the lie that what we have to offer
isn't worth sharing or is too much like
what's already out there. We are not copies;
we're one-of-a-kind creations. Amen.*

We look at books on shelves. We listen to songs on the radio. We watch speakers at events. And we can be tempted to ask, "How is there room for me, for what I have to offer, for the gifts I want to share?" It can feel as though everything worth doing has already been done. As wise Solomon said, there's nothing new under the sun. But here's the secret: it's not about what you do–it's about being YOU.

We've never read *your* words.

We've never heard *your* song.

We've never listened to *your* message.

You are made in the image of God. And that means there's a part of who He is that only gets shown to the world through who you are. Like a little puzzle piece. What will you reveal? If you don't let it show, we'll never know.

There's room for you. Dare to step into that space, your place. No one else can. No one else ever will. We need you just as you are.

You Are *Seen*

Indeed, the hairs of your head are
all counted. Don't be afraid; you are
worth more than many sparrows.

LUKE 12:7

*God, sometimes it seems as though what's most
visible is what's most valuable. But that isn't how
Your kingdom works, that is never Your heart
toward us. You see the small, hidden moments
of our lives. You hear our whispered prayers.
You know us and You notice us. When we're tempted
to feel invisible remind us that this is true:
we are always seen by You. Amen.*

The sun slips behind the spring trees exploding green. The birds declare love and war from the tips of branches. My dog stares down a squirrel, daring it to take one more step along the fence. The firepit is just beginning to crackle to life, sparks of gold and orange scattering into ashes.

I lean back into my rocking chair and find a rhythm that matches my thoughts. I feel small today. Like one of the sparrows scurrying across the yard. Back and forth. Back and forth. It's hard to see what all the fuss is about.

Then I remember that just as I see that sparrow, I'm seen by a God who made me. Knows me. Calls my name above the treetops and within my heart. Yes, I'm small. But in God's eyes, size doesn't equal significance.

The One who spun the stars onto the floor of the sky like dancers in evening gowns does not consider me of little importance. The One who watches seeds sleep beneath the earth's surface and then unfold into glory has a different point of view.

I matter to Him.

You do too.

You're Going to Be Okay

In God's eyes, SIZE doesn't equal

significance.

—HOLLEY GERTH

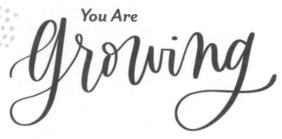

You Are *Growing*

So neither the one who plants nor the one
who waters is anything,
but only God, who makes things grow.

I CORINTHIANS 3:7 NIV

*God, we sometimes expect so much more from ourselves
than You do from us. You know we are human and that
as long as we're on this earth we'll still be in the process
of growth. Help us to be patient as You work in us,
to embrace the grace You so freely give us and to trust
that You will complete the good work You started in us.
We are not who we were yesterday and we are not
who we will be tomorrow, but now and always, we are loved.
Amen.*

We tell ourselves we have do it all, be it all, know it all right now. We deny ourselves the time and permission to really learn. And when we can't learn, we can't grow.

God doesn't judge or pressure us that way. He knows "all people are like grass, and all their glory is like the flowers of the field" (I Peter 1:24 NIV). I used to read that verse as simply meaning life is brief. But I'm seeing it with new eyes lately. And I think what God is also reminding us of here is that grass is growing, flowers are growing, *we* are growing.

Which means He knows that from our first breath to our last, we are in process. And that applies to everything from picking out curtains to becoming who He's created us to be.

And you know what? God's okay with that. He already knows us better than we know ourselves. If He's okay with it, then we can be too. He doesn't ask us for perfection, just growth. Every day, a little bit at a time, all the way until we're home with Him.

You are not who you were yesterday.

You are not who you will be tomorrow.

You're in the middle of the beautiful process of becoming.

You Don't Have to Feel Ready

I am sure of this, that He who started a
good work in you will carry it on to completion
until the day of Christ Jesus.

PHILIPPIANS 1:6

*God, thank You that being used by You
doesn't depend on our goodness, experience, education,
or qualifications. We can simply rely on You
and trust that You will work in and through us
for Your glory and the good of others. Give us
the courage to reach out, love, and freely
offer others what You've so generously given us.
Amen.*

I found myself the recipient of some unsolicited wisdom at a coffee shop this morning. A young man and his mentor sat next to me talking about faith and the young man asked, "When am I going to be ready to help someone else?"

The mentor paused and then answered, "I think you're asking the wrong question. Because as long as you ask 'Am I ready?' you'll always be able to find a reason you're not. A flaw. A struggle. Something you think you need to learn more about. The better question to ask is, 'Have I received something?' If so, then you have something to share. When is the best time to start passing it on? Yesterday."

God is not looking for perfect examples. He's looking for ordinary people who will love each other. He's calling the messy, the broken, and the incomplete. This is good news for all of us. It means our role is not to show off; it's just to show up. He will give to us and then He'll give through us. We're simply asked to be willing and brave enough to do it as we are and not as we'd like to be.

Strong, Brave, Loved

You Don't Have to *Compete*

Therefore, since we are surrounded by such a huge crowd
of witnesses to the life of faith, let us strip off every weight
that slows us down, especially the sin that so easily
trips us up. And let us run with endurance the race
God has set before us. We do this by keeping our eyes
on Jesus, the champion who initiates and perfects our faith.

HEBREWS 12:1–2 NLT

*God, when we hear life is a race, it can sound like it's all about
winning and losing, about comparing and competing.
But what You're really inviting us into is an intimate adventure
with You. It's not about being the fastest but about being faithful.
It's not about beating anyone else but about matching the rhythm
of our lives to the beating of Your heart.
Help us to run with and for You every step until we're Home.
Amen.*

We're all running a race, but not the kind you might imagine. We don't have the same starting line, the same distance to go, or the same steps to take. Our finish lines are even in different places. We're not running on a track—we're each running on our own one-lane path.

In God's kingdom, there's no such thing as competition. It's impossible. Because no one else ever has or ever will run your race. Your journey is about you and Jesus. No one else. He is not holding a stopwatch. He is not telling you to push harder. He is inviting you to move at the pace you're created for, to simply stay in step with Him. You will not fall behind. You will not move too slow. Keep your eyes off the other runners and fix them on the One who has invited You to this adventure with Him.

Take your next step today, then another one tomorrow. Keep pressing forward. Let go of what's behind. Be strong, brave, beautiful *you* all the way to the finish line.

Be strong,
brave,
beautiful
YOU.

—HOLLEY
GERTH

You Are Beautiful

God has made everything
beautiful for its own time.

ECCLESIASTES 3:11 NLT

God, our world has so many opinions on beauty,
but "the LORD does not look at the things people look at.
People look at the outward appearance,
but the LORD looks at the heart" (1 Samuel 16:7 NIV).
What matters about us isn't based on a mirror;
it's based on our Maker. You have created each of us
uniquely in Your image. We are Your works of art. Give us
the courage to believe that who we are is beautiful.
Amen.

I compare what I see in the mirror to the standards our culture puts out there for us as women. Am I thin enough? Is my make-up done right? Is my hair okay?

I think of how the Psalmist says that we're knit together in our mother's wombs (Psalm 139:13). What if we chose to see ourselves differently—the way God sees us? What if we asked God for His perspective—for His help with understanding the purpose for each feature He's given us?

He says we're wonderfully made. A divine design. A work of art. Who you are and how you look is intentional. Chosen with care. So let's be gentle with ourselves and with each other. We're God's beautiful daughters and, just like any parent, He delights in seeing us be fully and freely who we are.

It is said beauty is in the eye of the beholder. I'm learning to say beauty is in the eye of the Creator.

You Are
One-of-a-Kind

I praise you because of the
wonderful way you created me.

PSALM 139:14 CEV

God, this world tries to tell us we need to be more
like someone else, perhaps a celebrity, an athlete,
or the person at church who seems so much
more spiritual. But You only ask us to become
more like Jesus. You will make that happen
uniquely through each of us. When we feel
pressure to conform, help us to go instead to the
cross and remember that we are already
loved and accepted just the way we are.
Amen.

There has never been and will never be another you. That means the bravest thing you can do is to be who you already are. It can seem safer to be like someone else. It's easier to hide. It's simpler to say, "I'm not good enough," and walk away. But we need you.

We need your gifts.

We need your strengths.

We need your smile.

When you are who you're created to be, you become a mirror of the heart of the One who made you. The enemy of your soul will try to convince you to change who you are, because he loves to interfere with your reflection. Say no, my friend.

No to comparing.

No to competing.

No to copying.

Instead, open your heart, spread out your wings, lift up your head, and live with divine confidence. You have much to offer. You are a one-of-a-kind original. No one can ever be better at being you than you. Let's say yes together.

Yes to boldness.

Yes to beauty.

Yes to being who God made us.

Let's say "yes" with all our heart for all our life. Speak "yes" with everything we are and all that we become. Because one of the very best ways to change the world is by refusing to change who God created each of us to be.

You Are Provided for by God

God will supply all your needs according
to His riches in glory in Christ Jesus.

PHILIPPIANS 4:19

God, You are the giver of all that's good,
the meeter of our needs, the satisfier of our hearts.
You are not withholding from us. Instead You are
holding out Your hand to us and promising
that we will receive all that we need. When it seems
we don't have enough, help us to trust that You
will take care of us and You are working on our behalf
to bless us in ways beyond what we can see.
Amen.

God promises to provide for us. That doesn't mean we'll get everything we want. And the timing may be different than we imagine. What we have in mind may not match God's plan. But He will take care of us—no matter what.

God's part is to provide. Ours is to learn to be content in all circumstances (Philippians 4:12–13). I love that the apostle Paul uses the word "learn" in that passage. Birds seem to be born knowing how to trust their Maker. But for us it's a process. The more we discover who God is, the more we find that we can rely on Him to meet our needs. As we do, our striving is replaced by peace that passes understanding.

You are cared for more than you know, more than you see. So are the people in your life. You can be sure God knows all your needs. And He already has a way to provide for each one.

The Encouragement Project

God
knows

all your needs.

And He already has a way

to provide for each one.

—HOLLEY GERTH

You Are *More* than Your Hard Days

Do not fear, for I am with you; do not be afraid,
for I am your God. I will strengthen you; I will help you;
I will hold on to you with My righteous right hand.

ISAIAH 41:10

*God, sometimes our circumstances threaten to become
our identity. We start to believe we are defined
by our struggles. But nothing that happens today
can change who You say we are. Nothing can nullify
Your promises to us. Nothing can take away
what we have been given in You. On our worst days
remind us that You still have our best in mind.
You are still working everything together for our good.
Amen.*

Some days you will try your best and it will not feel like enough. Some days the words we want to bring healing will hurt instead. Some days we will question everything we do and why we do it.

This doesn't mean we're failures, we should quit, or God is disappointed in us. It just means that, for all our days, we will be human. All our days we will grow but not reach perfection. All our days there will be grace for us.

So let's keep going. Keep trying. Keep moving forward. I know it's hard on some days. But we are more than those days. And at the end of all our days we will hear, "Well done, good and faithful servant." That will make it all worthwhile.

Let's pause for a moment and remember we are loved.

Today. Tomorrow. Forever.

You Are God's *Friend*

I do not call you servants anymore,
because a servant doesn't know what his master
is doing. I have called you friends,
because I have made known to you
everything I have heard from My Father.

JOHN 15:15

*God, it's a stunning realization to know we can
call You "Friend." Your loyalty, care, and encouragement
make all the difference. Thank You for not keeping us
at a distance, but instead, wanting to be part of our lives
in an intimate, personal way. Please help us to be loyal,
faithful friends to You too.
Amen.*

When I consider what friendship really means, I think it comes down to this one thing: true friends are *for* us no matter what. They are not crossing their arms and saying, "I knew she couldn't do it." They are not passing the gossip along with the potato salad at the Sunday picnic. They are not wondering when we'll get over it, but instead, how they can walk with us through it.

When I think of Jesus being a Friend to us in these ways, it changes everything.

It's easy to think of Jesus as powerful, mighty, and holy. It's simpler for me to bend my knee than to dare to bend His ear about my daily, ordinary struggles. But we are His friends. We can go to Him with anything and everything. We can trust He'll be there to love, encourage, and support us.

Hope Your Heart Needs

You Are *Never* Inadequate

His divine power has given us everything required
for life and godliness through the knowledge of Him
who called us by His own glory and goodness.

II PETER 1:3

*God, when our to-do list feels long and our day feels short,
remind us that all we have to do is what You ask.
Free us from unrealistic expectations, from taking on
more than You ever ask, from wearing ourselves out
to prove our worth. Remind us we don't have to be adequate;
we only need to be obedient. Whatever little we
have to offer will be more than enough in Your hands.
Amen.*

I stare at the emails on my screen. I scan my daunting to-do list. I think of the many roles I want to fill well—wife, daughter, friend. I feel small. Not enough. Inadequate.

The reality is none of us are superwomen. Our ideal and our real never quite line up. Even with our best intentions, we fall short. We mess up. We let people down. And some days we're doing well just to get up in the morning.

But here's what God is gently showing me. In spite all that...

We are not inadequate.

We are in Christ.

This changes everything. Because Jesus makes up for what we lack. He fills the gaps. He multiplies our fish and loaves— whatever we have to offer. In Him we are enough. And we have enough.

We are never inadequate, because we always have a beyond-all-you-can-imagine God living in us.

We are
never
inadequate,
because we
always
have

a beyond-all-you-can-imagine

GOD

living in us.

—HOLLEY
GERTH

You Are *Victorious*

But thanks be to God,
who gives us the victory through
our Lord Jesus Christ!

I CORINTHIANS 15:57

*God, in this world we get knocked down.
We face battles and challenges. You understand
because You lived here too. But defeat
isn't our destiny. We're promised victory in You.
Strengthen our hearts, steady our feet,
give us everything we need to overcome
whatever we may face today.
Amen.*

You are already victorious. More than a conqueror. It may not feel that way in the heat of your battle, but you can be sure of this: the war is already won. You can't lose. You will not falter.

You have been promised that nothing can defeat you. Nothing. Not even what you are facing now. You can overcome as a warrior girl because you are mightier than you know. Your prayers, your unyielding faith, your words of truth have the power to make the enemy tremble. Not because of who you are but because of whose side you fight on.

And the One you fight with will always fight for you. He has done so since the beginning of time, and He will do so until every last obstacle and opposition has been destroyed. He is fierce on your behalf and infinitely tender with your heart.

Sometimes you will be wounded, yes. But don't let that trick you into believing you have been knocked down forever. That can never happen. Those wounds will be healed by the One whose scars have guaranteed victory for you.

Keep fighting. Refuse to let fear win. Never yield an inch to the enemy. You stand on holy ground, and no one can take what's yours.

Not now. Not ever.

You've already won forever.

If We Could Have Coffee

You Don't Have to Do *More*

Cease striving and know that I am God.

PSALM 46:10 NASB

God, You created the world in seven days
and You have kept it spinning since.
You don't have trouble carrying out Your to-do lists.
When it's tempting to believe our worth
is based on what we do, remind us
that the only work You want from us
is to believe (John 6:29). We choose to trust You
and live in grace today.
Amen.

We all hear it at times… the whisper in our hearts that says, "You really should be doing more." It usually intrudes right in the middle of our ordinary. When we're washing dishes. Or changing diapers. Or driving to work in the morning.

A wise friend of mine says it's a dangerous lie because every time we tell ourselves we should be doing more, it leads to less…

Being less present where we are right now.

Less peace.

Less joy.

Less love for those who are right in front of us.

Can you trust that you're where you're supposed to be in this moment, doing what you're supposed to be doing? Yes, be open to new possibilities. Learn. Grow. Take steps forward. But say "no" to the lie that you must do more.

Let's take a deep breath, lean into grace, and live fully where we are today. God is already taking care of tomorrow (and He's the only One who can).

You Are *Here* for Such a Time as *This*

David...served God's purposes in his own generation.

ACTS 13:36 NIV

*God, You are Lord of the past, present,
and future. You hold all of history and
what will yet be in Your hands. You have placed us
right here, right now, for such a time as this.
Our lives are not accidents but divinely created
appointments. Give us the courage to serve You
faithfully in this generation and leave a legacy
that will last for many more to come.*

Amen.

You are here for such a time as this. You are called to offer what God has placed within you to our world right here, right now. No one else will live the exact amount of time you will, in the place you will, with the people whom God will have cross your path.

It's tempting to say, "Oh, I'm not really needed." But "we are God's handiwork, created in Christ Jesus to do good works, which God prepared in advance for us to do" (Ephesians 2:10 NIV). In other words, there are things in this world that only you can do.

For such a time as this...

You're changing diapers, tying the shoelaces of the future, growing the seeds of strong faith.

For such a time as this...

You're working in that office, speaking up in that meeting, doing what you do with excellence.

For such a time as this...

You're reaching out a helping hand, taking time to listen, brightening someone's day.

For such a time as this...

You are wherever you are, doing whatever you do, and it matters more than you know.

So keep it up.

You really are making a difference.

You are
HERE

for such a time as
THIS.

INSPIRED BY
ESTHER 4:14

You Are *Chosen*

For we know, brothers and sisters
loved by God, that He has chosen you.

I THESSALONIANS 1:4

*God, we are not here by accident, but by
Your design. Before we took our first breath
You knew us, and You have pursued us
every day of our lives. You chose us and we freely
and wholeheartedly choose You. We are Yours
and we want to do Your will today.*
Amen.

God called your name. He formed you with love in your mother's womb and intricately designed every part of who you would become. You truly are fearfully and wonderfully made—a masterpiece by the same God who spread the oceans farther than we can even see. He numbers every hair on your head. He knows every care in your heart. You belong to Him.

Your journey on this path is not by coincidence. You are here because God looked out over all of history and chose you for a particular time and purpose. You could have entered the world a hundred years ago or a thousand years from now. But you are in this generation, this time, and there will never be another you or another opportunity to do what only you are chosen to complete.

Go out in boldness knowing that you don't have to be like anyone else. You don't have to do what any other person has done. You are chosen for one life—yours.

You're Made for a God-Sized Dream

You Are Already
Approved

For we speak as messengers approved by God
to be entrusted with the Good News.
Our purpose is to please God, not people.
He alone examines the motives of our hearts.

1 THESSALONIANS 2:4 NLT

*God, our hearts long for approval, yet it's so easy to
believe it's something we have to earn rather than receive.
Right now, in this moment, we pause and take
a deep breath of grace. We remember that we belong
to You, we are forgiven and we have nothing to prove.
Help us to walk in the freedom of that today.
Amen.*

I remember grace is for eternity.

But I sometimes forget it's also for each day.

When I'm forgetful in that way, I slip into old patterns. I try too hard. I do too much. I listen to the whispers of guilt and shame. What my heart needs to recall is this: Grace is not a one-time offer. Yes, we first receive it when we become believers. But it's also a gift offered every moment after. It never runs out. Never.

Grace means we no longer need to earn God's approval. It is ours because of what Jesus did for us. It can't be lost.

So if you're feeling weary or exhausted today, it may be that you need to embrace God's grace all over again. You don't have to try so hard. You don't have to do so much. You don't have to worry so often about how you're measuring up.

All that really needs to be done in our lives was completed when Jesus said, "It is finished," on the cross (John 19:30).

We are covered by grace. We are approved. We are always loved.

You Are
Beyond Compare

Now there are different gifts, but the same Spirit.
There are different ministries, but the same Lord.
And there are different activities, but the same God
produces each gift in each person.

I CORINTHIANS 12:4–6

*God, You are our Creator and You made each one of us
just as You wanted us to be. When You look at us You don't
compare us to each other—help us to do the same. Give us eyes
that recognize our strengths without pride, that see each other's
gifts without envy, that have a vision for how we are better
together because we are all different and all deeply loved.*

Amen.

Before you took your first breath, God placed gifts within you. He wove you together with strengths, abilities, and that smile of yours that lights up a room. He made you irreplaceable. There's one thing no other person in the world can do better than you, and that's simply being you.

You are made in the image of God, and there's a part of who He is that only shows up in this world through you. You may feel ordinary. But you are a masterpiece. A bit of the divine. Extraordinary.

When you let your heart receive that, believe it, live it, then you're simply agreeing with God. That's not pride. It's actually the greatest humility to say, "Yes, God, I affirm that all You made is good—and that includes me."

And not only did He form you before you were born, but He also made you a new creation when you gave your life to Jesus. Not simply a new person—a new creation.

In other words, a completely unique being. Here's why that matters: If there's only one of something, it can't be compared. You're not compared by God to anyone else, and that means you don't have to compare yourself to others either.

If We Could Have Coffee

You are made
in the
image of
GOD,

and there's

a

 *part of*

who He is

that only shows up in this world

through YOU.

—HOLLEY GERTH

You Are
Wanted

But you are a chosen race, a royal priesthood,
a holy nation, a people for His possession, so that
you may proclaim the praises of the one who called you
out of darkness into His marvelous light.

I PETER 2:9

*God, sometimes we can believe the lie that we're
not wanted. We're left off the team, overlooked for the
project, or not invited to the party. But You whisper
to us always, "I choose you." This is a beautiful mystery.
On the days when we feel alone help us to lean in
and listen to Your voice above all others.
We are never unwanted; we are always loved.
Amen.*

I scroll through the photos of adopted children. Each one has a caption below it with a message from the parents who chose them. The phrases jump out at me...

"The best gift ever."

"We are blessed that we could adopt her."

"She has brought so much joy to our lives."

While every adoption story is different, they all have this in common: adoption is about choice and celebration, not obligation.

It takes my breath away to think that's how God sees His relationship with us as well. Ephesians 1:5 (NLT) says, "God decided in advance to adopt us into His own family by bringing us to Himself through Jesus Christ. This is what He wanted to do, and it gave Him great pleasure." God wanted us. He pursued us. He delighted in making us His forever.

And His affection for us isn't based on anything we do. Adoption isn't earned—it's received. Those kids didn't win their parents over by being perfect. They weren't selected because they were the "best" at something. They didn't get a family as a reward for following a list of rules.

I look again at the page with the adoption photos. There's so much light in the eyes of those parents. So much love in their smiles. Their children clearly bring them joy simply because they are their children. Can we dare to believe that's how God feels about us too?

We are wanted—today and forever.

You Are *Loved* No Matter What

God is love, and the one who remains in love
remains in God, and God remains in him. In this,
love is made complete with us.... There is no fear
in love; instead, perfect love drives out fear.

1 JOHN 4:16–18

*God, You are the only One who loves us perfectly
and completely. On the days when we don't feel
Your love, remind us that it is still always there.
We are Yours forever, and nothing can ever separate us
from the love we have in You. We don't deserve it,
we don't have to earn it, we can never lose it.
You are God. We are loved. That is forever true.
Amen.*

People will never love us perfectly. And when they don't, it's easy to assume it's our fault. We tell ourselves, "I'll try harder to be perfect so I can be loved." But that's a treadmill that will lead us nowhere except to burnout and frustration.

Yes, we do need perfect love. But we can only get it from one place: God's heart. If we see Him as demanding, demeaning, or simply apathetic, then we'll keep running toward other sources. Every quest for perfection has at its root some incorrect belief about how God loves us. We pick up those lies from all kinds of places without even realizing it.

We can ask God to show us where we've accidentally accepted what isn't true and replace it with what our heart really needs instead. We don't have to live in fear anymore. Instead we can say by faith...

God is for you.

God is with you.

God loves you beyond all you can even imagine. Right here. Right now. As you are.

You're Loved No Matter What

You Don't Have to Be Like Anyone *Else*

God saw all that He had made,
and it was very good.

GENESIS 1:31

*God, comparison is a joy-stealer that tries to take
what You freely give us: holy confidence,
freedom to be who You've made us,
and unconditional love that heals our hearts.
When we're tempted to compare, help us cling
to the truth of who You say we are instead.
We choose to believe that we are who
You made us to be, and we are better together.
Amen.*

I walk through my home, thoughts swirling through my mind like the dust bunnies doing dances in front of my vacuum. I think of other women who have cleaner houses. Which leads to thoughts of those who cook better meals. And that goes on to the ones who have cuter outfits, and are better at social media, and can make small talk with ease.

I wish I could be like… is the refrain that goes round and round in my mind.

Finally, feeling drained, I hit the power button on the vacuum.

I whisper a question, "God, why do I feel the need to be like so many other people?"

It seems there is an answer that comes so quiet…

Because the enemy would rather have you be like anyone but Jesus.

If I'm busy trying to be like Mary, Martha, and Margaret, then I'm left with no time to be me. Or, more specifically, to let Jesus be who He is through me. Each of us are made in the image of God. That means we're created to show Him to the world in a way no one else ever has and no one else ever will.

I do that by being who He made me.

And you do that by being you.

I empty the vacuum bag into the garbage and admire how dust and clutter give way to clean again. I smile because my heart suddenly feels like that too. Comparison replaced by clarity—about who I am, what I'm called to do, and the God who's wild enough to choose me for His purposes.

Each of us are made in the

image of
GOD.

—HOLLEY GERTH

You Are an Overcomer

In all these things we are more than
conquerors through Him who loved us.

ROMANS 8:37

God, in this world we will face battles.
We will have struggles. There will be blood, sweat,
and tears. But whatever we may face, You promise
that we can and will overcome it with You. Give us
the strength to keep fighting, the courage never
to give up, and the faith to stand firm
no matter what happens. We entrust ourselves
to You, the One who will deliver us.
Amen.

There is nothing you will face this week that's bigger than your God. No problem. No struggle. No opposition. He can't be defeated and therefore you can't be defeated either. Yes, there may be some battles. You may even be wounded. But you will not be overcome.

He is in the hospital room when the test results come. He is in the meeting when the announcement is made. He is in your living room when the person you love slams the front door and walks into the night. He is there in the middle of it all, standing with you on the battlefield, promising You that the war isn't over, the enemy will not win in the end.

It's okay to let the tears stream down your face, to pound your fists against your pillow, to feel tired and sad and confused. In the middle of it all, just hold tightly to what's true and refuse to let anyone or anything take it from you. You're stronger than you feel right now. And our God is even more powerful than you can imagine. With Him on our side, victory is sure.

You Can

Defeat

Fear

Be strong, and let your heart be courageous,
all you who put your hope in the LORD.

PSALM 31:24

*God, we all have moments when we
feel weak, when we might be overwhelmed
or overcome by life. But we won't be
because You are our strength, and nothing
is impossible for You. Knowing this, we will
not give in, give up, or back down. Instead we will
press on, keep fighting, and claim the victory
that is already ours because of You.
Amen.*

I'm driving home after having lunch with a new friend, replaying the conversation. Fear makes my breathing shallow, my heartbeat fast. What if she doesn't like me? What if I came across all wrong? I often have moments like this when anxiety gets the best of me and I want to retreat from the whole world.

But this time I pray, "Jesus, help me. I don't understand why I act this way. I want to be free from this struggle." A simple declaration comes to my heart: I am done running away. From now on, I am running toward.

I don't even fully understand what this means, but when I get home, I put on my tennis shoes. I walk out the door and onto the trail behind our house. I turn on my favorite music and run like my life depends on it. *No more, no more, no more,* I say with every step.

I think of all I have run away from... how fear has chased me and people-pleasing has set my pace, how anxiety has nipped at my heels like a rogue chihuahua, how the lies have worn me out.

I am done.

I will no longer be a woman who's defined or controlled by what she's running from.

I am going to run toward grace. I am going to run toward love. I am going to run toward the wild dreams that beckon me in the distance. I am going to run toward boldness and freedom and holy confidence. I am going to run toward Jesus.

I finish, sweaty and spent on the outside, strong and roaring on the inside. I don't know everything this new perspective means, what exactly I have done. But it feels as though something dark and destructive challenged me to a race today.

And I won.

You Can Be
Confident

Now faith is confidence in what we hope for
and assurance about what we do not see.

HEBREWS 11:1 NIV

God, this world tells us we need more self-esteem,
but what we really need is holy confidence.
This means recognizing we are Your creation,
You have given us strengths and gifts to share,
and You have a purpose for us only we can fulfill.
When insecurity lies to us, bring us back
to the truth of who we are and Whose we are.
You alone determine our identity and destiny.
Amen.

"Wait," I say to my husband, "read that part again." It's early morning and I think I must have misheard the Scripture he just finished.

He repeats, "Faith is confidence..." (Hebrews 11:1 NIV).

Huh. I heard right after all. Of course faith is the secret of confidence. Why had I never made the connection between those two before?

I tend to think of faith as external while confidence comes from within. But isn't that where faith really comes from too? From our hearts and the One who dwells within them?

I lean back on the couch and sip my coffee. It feels like a big moment. Because this changes everything. It means not only can I be confident, but it's also part of faith.

This kind of confidence isn't based on our humanity—it's based on who God is, who He created us to be, and the eternal plan He's working out in this world every day.

I can be confident.

You can be confident.

We can walk through this world with heads and hearts held high as Daughters of the King (who wear pajama pants and sometimes don't get up on time).

Let's dare to live with greater faith and confidence. Right here. Right now. And forever.

FAITH *is*

confidence...

HEBREWS 11:1 NIV

Your Brokenness Is Part of Your

Beauty

The LORD is near the brokenhearted;
He saves those crushed in spirit.

PSALM 34:18

*God, You were broken on a cross so that we
could be made whole. You mysteriously use our hurts
to bring comfort and healing to others.
You take what we might see as pointless pain
and turn it into eternal gain.
This doesn't mean what we go through isn't hard,
but it does mean there is hope. Please take
all of what we've been through and redeem it,
restore it, make it beautiful for You.
Amen.*

As I drove home from work one day, the pain I felt seemed especially pointless, and in turn, my life did too. "God," I whispered, "how can You use me when I'm so broken?" A song came on the radio that repeated a verse from Isaiah over and over again:

> He was pierced for our transgressions,
>
> He was crushed for our iniquities;
>
> the punishment that brought us peace was on Him,
>
> and by His wounds we are healed (Isaiah 53:5).

I started singing along with the words. As I did it seemed God whispered to my soul, "You think you have to take what's broken and make it perfect in order to be used by Me. But I think in a completely different way. I took what was perfect, My Son, and made Him broken so that you could be whole. And because you belong to Him, your brokenness can bring healing to others too."

It's a crazy, upside-down way of thinking. But it's true. God has used my brokenness in ways I never expected. It's become part of who I am, a surprisingly beautiful part. He doesn't just restore; He transforms. Beauty from ashes—or brokenness.

You're Already Amazing

You Don't Have to Be "*Fine*"

Then they cried out to the LORD in their trouble;
He rescued them from their distress.

PSALM 107:6

God, You tell us that we don't have to do life alone.
It can be hard to admit that we need help
but doing so isn't ever weakness; it's an act of bravery.
Give us the courage to say, "I'm not okay"
and to listen with grace and compassion
when others say the same to us. Because of You
none of us need to have life all together;
we only need to remember we're better together.
Amen.

A friend of mine recently went through a difficult time, and as several of us gathered around her to offer support, she kept saying, "I'm not allowed to be broken." How many of us have felt that way? I certainly have.

This friend is incredibly kind and generous. If you need anything, she's there. So we gently asked, "How does it make you feel when you help us?" She looked up with tears in her eyes and said, "It's good. It makes me feel valued and loved." We responded, "Then give us the gift of helping you now."

This is the incorrect belief we have to change: If we need help, we're a burden. Because the opposite is true. In the kingdom of God, it's more of a blessing to give than receive. So don't deprive those around you of those benefits just because you're afraid of what they may think of you.

Let's give others the gift of helping us. We need it—and they need to see we're not perfect, because it sets them free to ask for help and grace too.

You Are *Never* a Failure

Yes, and I am willing to look
even more foolish than this,
even to be humiliated in my own eyes!

II SAMUEL 6:22 NLT

God, You don't define success in the way
this world does. With You, success is about
love and obedience, not external results.
Thank You that our value and identity
don't depend on our achievements
or what others think or say about us.
You alone get the final word on our worth.
Amen.

Noah built an ark.

Moses wandered in the desert.

Jesus hung on the cross.

And some of those who watched shook their heads and muttered words like "failure" and "fool."

Little did they know.

Have you stepped out in faith and wondered why you feel like a fool? Have you come across failure like a roadblock in your path? Keep going. Instead of fleeing from the feeling of being foolish, lean into it.

King David did this when the Ark of God entered Jerusalem. He danced in joy, with lots of abandon and little clothing, all in front of the people. His wife scolded him for what she saw as inappropriate behavior for a person of his position. I love his response: "Yes, and I am willing to look even more foolish than this, even to be humiliated in my own eyes!" Where most of us would apologize and try to defend ourselves, David essentially says: "You ain't seen nothing yet." He realizes that defending his honor is not his job and that God gets the most glory when we humble ourselves.

Let's never give up, give in, compromise, or quit. We're going to make it. And it's going to make us... not into fools, not into failures, but into victorious followers.

Opening the Door to Your God-Sized Dream

You alone get
the final word
on our worth.
Amen.

—HOLLEY GERTH

You Really Are
Forgiven

Love...does not keep a record of wrongs.

1 CORINTHIANS 13:4–5

*God, Your grace is beyond our comprehension.
We don't deserve it and yet You extravagantly
offer it to us each moment of every day.
When shame and guilt try to tell us that we
aren't really forgiven, that it isn't really over,
remind us of what You said on the cross:
"It is finished." Nothing we have done will ever
be bigger or stronger than what You did for us.
Amen.*

I messed up. Again. I sat on the back deck thinking about what a failure I'd been. What must God think of me? I began to write about my mistake. I finished and looked at the black-and-white evidence that I had fallen short yet again. Then I seemed to hear a whisper in my heart.

"Rip out the page." I paused and listened closer. "Rip out the page."

"God, what are You saying? What do You mean, rip out the page? I need to record this mistake. I need to remember it."

Again the clear message came. "Rip out the page."

I touched the white page of my journal, now covered with writing. Then slowly I pulled from top to bottom.

I realized at that moment that God loves me. He doesn't just tolerate me. He doesn't just put up with me because I'm a Christian and He has to. He really, truly loves me.

So wherever you are, whatever mistake you have written in the journal of your life, know that God has ripped it from the pages.

There's only love.

There's only grace.

The story of your life is far different than you imagined... and the Author loves you far more than you ever dared to dream.

You're Already Amazing

You Are
Called

God is faithful;
you were called by Him into fellowship
with His Son, Jesus Christ our Lord.

I CORINTHIANS 1:9

*God, it's amazing to know that You have
called us. You've chosen us. You've given us a part
in Your plan. Out of all of history, this is the time
and place You wanted us to be. Help us
to see Your extraordinary plan even in the middle
of our most ordinary days. Where You are
is holy ground and You are always with us.*

Amen.

You're here on earth for far more than just to take up space. God doesn't want you to just "survive" until you get home to heaven where life truly begins. When we know Him, eternity begins now. Your days are significant, and He has no intention of wasting them. We've often relegated the word *calling* to specifically spiritual vocations, like being a pastor. But the reality is, we all have unique tasks we're asked to do throughout our lives.

This means that what you do every day matters. Your life has significance. God describes Himself as "I AM" (Exodus 3:14). I love that because it's present tense. It's right here and now. If God is always with us, then there are no ordinary moments in our lives. Wherever you are right now, you are standing on holy ground.

Your life matters. You have significance. You are called.

You're Made for a God-Sized Dream

You Are Enough

My grace is sufficient for you,
for my power is perfected in weakness.

II CORINTHIANS 12:9

God, thank You that through what Jesus did
on the cross, You "forever made perfect those
who are being made holy" (Hebrews 10:14 NLT).
On the days when we think we have to make
ourselves perfect through our own efforts, remind us
we are already positionally perfect in You—
You are making us more like Jesus every day
through Your Spirit. What You want from us
is not perfection, but growth and connection.
Amen.

Like most women, I can relentlessly push myself to be and do more. Deep inside, I also live with the lie that says I am not "enough."

But I'm coming to understand that being enough in God's kingdom does not mean having status, wealth, or stunning beauty. It's an entirely different perspective from what the world sees as enough. In God's eyes, we are enough because He is enough in us. He promises to give us "everything we need for life" (II Peter 1:3 NIV). Not everything we want—but everything we need. Including who we need to be to fulfill His unique purpose for our lives.

We often feel as if we have to strive for love and acceptance. Yet God invites us to come to Him and believe that, no matter what the world may try to tell us, no matter which lies have wounded our hearts, no matter how inadequate we may feel at times, we are already enough.

In God's eyes,

WE

are enough

because

HE

is enough
in us.

—HOLLEY
GERTH

You'll Have the

Wisdom

You Need

If you need wisdom, ask our generous God,
and He will give it to you.
He will not rebuke you for asking.

JAMES 1:5 NLT

*God, it's such a relief to know we don't have to
figure everything out, we only need to come
to You in faith trusting You'll provide the answers
we need. You do that in many ways—through
Your Word, Your Spirit, other people— but You
are always the source. You will not let us
dwell in confusion, but instead give us clarity and
confidence for every decision and circumstance.
Amen.*

What exactly is wisdom? I believe it's seeing the world, and our specific situations, through God's eyes. It's having His perspective, a deeper knowledge of what's happening than we can get just from our five senses. Often it's contradictory to what looks like the right answers. Instead, it's the real answer. Wisdom does more than just provide solutions; it leads to breakthroughs.

Walking in wisdom takes faith and courage. It can't often be justified with a spreadsheet or measured with numbers. It has to be lived and experienced. When someone needs wisdom, they also need the boldness to step forward without knowing all the answers ahead of time. Wisdom is often given to us as we go, one step at a time.

The great news is that God promises to give us the wisdom we need. All we have to do is ask and have the humility to receive the response, even if it's not what we expected. You have the God who knows absolutely everything living within you. And whoever you're praying for now is known by Him too. There's no problem too complex, no circumstance too confusing, no situation too overwhelming for Him. He's already got the answer. Even better, He *is* the answer.

The Encouragement Project

You Are
Stronger
than You Feel
Right Now

I am able to do all things
through Him who strengthens me.

PHILIPPIANS 4:13

*God, it sometimes feels like we need to be strong—
to put on a smile, a brave face—and do what needs
to be done. But You tell us Your strength is made
perfect in weakness, which means the moments
when we feel the least spiritual might just be the ones
when You work most. Because it's in those times
we're reminded that we can depend fully and
completely on You. It's not about being strong;
it's about letting You be our strength.
Amen.*

Sometimes what's in front of us seems impossible. The hill is too steep. The test is too hard. The diagnosis is too discouraging. But Jesus says to us, "Whatever I ask you to go through, I will give you the strength to do."

When we're weary, He's our power.

When we're afraid, He's our courage.

When we're uncertain, He's our security.

After a difficult day I woke in the night with one verse on my heart: "Not by strength or by might, but by My Spirit" (Zechariah 4:6). I needed a reminder that the outcome isn't based on what I can offer in my humanity. Instead, I can trust in the God who has promised to get me through whatever I may face. It is not my strength that matters—it's His strength flowing through me by the power of His Spirit.

Nothing is too much for us, because nothing we will ever face is bigger than the God who lives within us. He already knows what we're going to face today. And He's already promised us we're going to beat it—no matter what.

You Are
Accepted

Therefore accept one another, just as Christ
also accepted you, to the glory of God.

ROMANS 15:7

*God, it's so easy to try to earn approval by being good,
by trying harder, or by making everyone happy.
Thank You that we don't have to do that because we're
already accepted and approved through what
Jesus did for us on the cross. We've been made right
with You, and Your love empowers us to
share acceptance and approval with others too.
Amen.*

We don't have to prove ourselves. We have already been declared "approved" by God. Not because of how good we are, but because of what Jesus did for us on the cross. All the laws, all the expectations, were nailed there with Him. And when He rose again three days later, we were declared to be free forever.

You are accepted. I am accepted. And love is no longer a reward for our behavior but instead a gift offered by nail-scarred hands. So let's drop the lists we're clutching and cling to what He longs to bring to our lives instead.

Wherever you are right now, take a deep, slow breath. Let it out again, and as you do, think of all those expectations slipping away too.

Every "I should..."

Each "I must..."

All the "I have to's..."

Replace them instead with this:

"Because Jesus loves me, I will..."

"Because He fully accepts me, I can..."

"Because He promises me everything I need, I get to..."

When we live that way, our expectations are exchanged for exclamations—declarations from deep within our hearts and lives that tell the world we serve a God of grace.

If We Could Have Coffee

We don't have to prove ourselves.

We have

already

been declared

"approved"

by

GOD.

—HOLLEY GERTH

You Are Never *Alone*

Remember, I am with you always,
to the end of the age.

MATTHEW 28:20

*God, our world is more connected than
ever before, and yet underneath all the
social media and small talk we can feel alone.
In those moments, remind us of Your presence
with us, draw us close to Your heart again,
let us know You're with us always.
No matter how we may feel, we are never,
ever alone because of You.
Amen.*

We all have moments when we feel alone. In a world where everyone seems to be connected, it seems ironic that studies show we're more isolated than ever before. That sense of separateness can create cracks where lies slip into our hearts.

Lies that say, "Everyone has more friends than you."

Lies that taunt, "Maybe you don't really belong here."

Lies that even accuse, "If anyone really knew you, you wouldn't be loved the same."

Can we shudder together at the ugliness of those words? And then can we say as sisters that we won't listen to them anymore?

You are not alone. I am not alone. Even in the moments when we feel like we are.

God has promised He is with us, He is for us, and He will never leave us. Yesterday, today, and forever we are surrounded by more love than we can see, feel, or even imagine.

Your Tears
Matter
to God

You keep track of all my sorrows.
You have collected all my tears in Your bottle.
You have recorded each one in Your book.

PSALM 56:8 NLT

*God, thank You for the gift of tears; for a way
to let our emotions show and flow in the hard
moments. You aren't telling us to keep things together,
instead You're keeping us close to Your heart—
especially when we're hurting. You're our comfort
and our hope, our help and strength,
the caretaker of our tears and all that concerns us.
Our sorrow is safe with You.
Amen.*

If you could read a record of your tears, what would it contain? You probably can't even remember each one you've shed or why. But it seems God does. David trusts that all of his tears are in God's record. Why do we write things down? Because we want to remember. Because they are important to us. Because they tell a story. Perhaps all of these are reasons why God keeps our tears in His record. It's His way of telling us, "Your tears are not just water and salt to Me. They are part of who you are. I value them because I love you."

God gives attention to our tears. In doing so, He affirms that it's okay to cry. Yes, even the mascara-smearing, snot-dripping kind of cry. I think God sees extraordinary beauty in our ugly cry. That kind of crying is what it looks like when a human heart is laid bare and open. It's what we do when we stop trying so hard to be strong. It's our way of saying, "This is too much for me." It's—dare I say it—an act of worship because we finally let ourselves be humans who need God.

So go ahead and let loose. Cry when you're sad. Cry when you're happy. Cry when you're angry. Let's dare to tell the story of our lives through our tears and remember that God, the Author of life, is treasuring each one.

What Your Heart Needs for the Hard Days

You Have a *Purpose*

I cry out to God Most High,
to God who will fulfill His purpose for me.
PSALM 57:2 NLT

*God, our lives are not random or by chance.
We are created and called by You. When it seems
our plans go wrong, when our circumstances
don't make sense, when we can't see what's next,
remind us that You are in control, and there is
a greater purpose behind it all. Give us the courage
to trust You, to place ourselves in Your hands
even when we don't understand.
Amen.*

The question, "What is my purpose?" comes to our hearts in unexpected moments during our lives. We long to believe our time here on earth is significant. And we often look to people or positions to help us fill the void that lingers as we search for answers. But still the question in our souls remains.

This morning two verses caught my attention: "The Pharisees and the experts in the law rejected God's purpose for themselves." (Luke 7:30 NIV). In contrast, "David had served God's purpose in his own generation" (Acts 13:36 NIV).

What's the difference? The Pharisees and teachers of the law insisted on living their way. By their rules. Their standards. Their righteousness. But David was a man who chose to live God's way. The Pharisees were focused on appearing to do big things for God. David was intent on spending every little moment of life with God.

In other words, it turns out our purpose is actually a Person. Our reason for being is God Himself. Living with purpose simply means living with God. We don't have to find our purpose someday, somewhere. Instead we can simply love the One who loves us right now, right here.

Living
with purpose

simply means living *with* GOD.

—HOLLEY GERTH

You Are Going to Be *Okay*

I will be with you when you pass through the waters,
and when you pass through the rivers, they will
not overwhelm you. You will not be scorched when you
walk through the fire, and the flame will not burn you.

ISAIAH 43:2

*God, sometimes life is hard and it hurts. In those
moments, help us to turn to You. We need
Your peace. We need Your strength. We need
Your hope to help us see that there are better days ahead.
Because of You we will make it through.
Because of You we're going to be okay.
Amen.*

No matter what you're facing, no matter how hard it seems, no matter how much you feel like giving up on some days, *hold on.*

You're going to be okay.

Not because life is easy.

Not because you have it all together.

Not because everything will work out the way you want.

You're going to make it through this because of who you are and Who you belong to.

You are a woman of strength. You are a daughter of the King. You are made for a Promised Land. And one day you'll be Home. You'll be with the One you love forever. Then you'll hear those words you've longed for: "Well done, good and faithful servant; you were faithful over a few things, I will make you ruler over many things. Enter into the joy of your Lord'" (Matthew 25:21 NKJV).

Can you hear the whisper of it even now? Lean in close and listen one more time to what's true... You are a woman who is loved. You are a woman who brings joy. You are a woman who's really going to be okay.

You're Going to Be Okay

You *Can* Do This

Jesus said, "With man it is impossible,
but not with God,
because all things are possible with God."

MARK 10:27

*God, there is nothing we can't do because of You.
So when the hill seems too steep, the mountain too high,
the river too wide, draw us back to Your side. Remind us
that You spoke the world into being, You scattered the stars
into place, You split the sea open wide. You are
the miracle-working, way-making God, and You are
not done yet. Whatever You're asking us to do, we say "yes"
to You today. You will make a way. You are the way.
Amen.*

I sit on the back porch and stare out over open space. The scene is serene but inside my mind it's a far different landscape. I think of all that's ahead of me, then I whisper the words, "I don't know if I can do this."

"I don't know if I have the strength."

"I don't know if I have the perseverance."

"I don't know if I have the wisdom."

Have you ever felt that way too?

Thankfully when Jesus said we could do all things through Him, it included *this*. It included *right now*.

We don't have to be strong, because He says, "I will strengthen you and help you" (Isaiah 41:10 NIV).

We don't have to do this alone, because He promises, "I will be with you...because I love you" (Isaiah 43:2–4 NIV).

We don't have to figure everything out, because He assures us, "I will...teach you in the way you should go" (Psalm 32:8 NIV).

This is the secret that can empower us on the days when we feel overwhelmed, the truth we can hold on to when we get discouraged. The wild mystery that lifts life's weight from our shoulders says: It's not about *what* we have in us; it's about *Who*. Nothing is impossible for God—which means that with Him, nothing is impossible for us too.

You Are in
God's Care

Give all your worries and cares
to God, for He cares about you.

I PETER 5:7 NLT

God, thank You for so graciously taking
our burdens, fears, and anxieties.
Nothing is too heavy for You to carry,
and nothing is too hard for You to bear
on our behalf. We choose to
release what's been weighing us down
into Your loving hands.
Amen.

The word *anxiety* in I Peter 5:7 means more than I originally thought. It's not just that fluttery feeling in our chests, not just the worry that barks at us in the night. It describes any trouble or difficulty, any challenge or hardship, all the fears and uncertainties. Every bit of it.

I write these words about releasing our cares, knowing this is more easily said than done. I have a nervous system that leans toward stress. My fear circuits are sensitive. Sometimes it seems I battle worry all the time, every day. Do I always immediately hand over my cares? No. Often I carry them until I simply can't anymore, until they slip from my shoulders because I'm flat-out exhausted and can't take another step. But you know what? Jesus takes them even then. And I am learning, slowly, to let go sooner.

Knowing Jesus is my caretaker isn't an easy fix. It's not a simple one-time solution. For me, this truth means there is always hope. It means I'm discovering a different, freer way of being. It means I'm believing that by the time I reach my final destination, I will be traveling so much lighter.

Hope Your Heart Needs

give all your worries and cares to GOD,

for He cares about

YOU.

I PETER 5:7 NLT

You Are Making a

Difference

You are the light of the world—
like a city on a hilltop that cannot be hidden.

MATTHEW 5:14 NLT

*God, You are Lord of what's invisible and eternal,
what our eyes can't see, our ears can't hear,
and our fingers can't touch.
Our limitations as humans can make us feel as
if we're not making a difference, but that isn't true—
it's just that Your ways aren't like ours. You are
working in and through us even when we can't see it.
Our role isn't results; it's simply obedience.
Grant us the courage to believe that today regardless
of what we may not see until eternity.
Amen.*

We will all have moments when we get to be on the front lines and witness how we make a difference. But we will also have many days when we must keep believing without seeing.

When we keep loving that rebellious child even though there's no sign of change.

When we practice integrity in our workplace even though no one else seems to notice.

When we type words in the quiet in the hopes they will speak to a hurting heart.

Just because we can't see, touch, or even feel something, it doesn't make it any less real. So when we question if what we do matters, when it seems as though God is calling others to something more important or spiritual, when we wonder if we're just fooling ourselves into believing this is where we're supposed to be: we can take heart.

Our invisible God is there with us. He is working through us. And He will use each of us in His own mysterious ways to change the world.

You Are
Needed

Just as there are many parts to our bodies,
so it is with Christ's body. We are all parts of it,
and it takes every one of us to make it complete,
for we each have different work to do. So we belong
to each other, and each needs all the others.

ROMANS 12:5 TLB

*God, You have ways for each of us to contribute
and make a difference. You've given us the gifts, strengths,
and skills we need to serve. Show us how to use
what You've entrusted to us, to be who You've created
us to be, and to do what You've asked us to do.
Thank You for including us in Your purposes and plans.
Amen.*

As I type these words, I'm wearing a green rubber bracelet engraved with four words: "Gitzen Girl" and "Choose Joy." Gitzen Girl, whose real name is Sara Frankl, went home to Jesus a few years ago after being homebound with illness even though she was only in her thirties. And yet from within her home's walls, she found a way to touch thousands of lives through her words. As she got ready to head home to Jesus, stories from all over the Internet poured out, and our eyes widened as we realized how impactful Sara's life had been—even more than we knew before. Knowing Sara changed me and my definition of limitations because she turned hers into opportunities.

Sara could have said, "I can't even leave my house. I'm not needed." Instead she shifted her focus to others and simply asked, "Who can I encourage today?" Sara's role in the body of Christ looked different than many others', and yet she beautifully and joyfully chose to fulfill it. We can all do the same.

You are irreplaceable. What other parts of the body of Christ are doing isn't better—just different. You have something to offer that no one else can, and that's you.

You're Made for a God-Sized Dream

You Don't Have to
Hurry *or* Hustle

Don't worry about anything; instead, pray
about everything. Tell God what you need,
and thank Him for all He has done.
Then you will experience God's peace,
which exceeds anything we can understand.
His peace will guard your hearts
and minds as you live in Christ Jesus.

PHILIPPIANS 4:6–7 NLT

God, slow us down to the pace You have for us. We don't
want to take a single step ahead of You. Turn our worry
into worship. Turn our striving into serving You.
Turn our pressure into freedom. It is only in You that
"we live and move and have our being" (Acts 17:28).
Amen.

I'm learning this simple, hard truth: I can't run at the world's pace and walk with God at the same time. Pastor and author John Ortberg once described the pace of his life to theologian Dallas Willard. John asked for spiritual insight and this was the reply from Dallas: "You must ruthlessly eliminate hurry from your life."

Yes, eliminating hurry has something to do with our calendars. But I think it has even more to do with our hearts. I rush into and through my day because I am afraid. And only Jesus can calm my fear. Only Jesus can remind me I don't have to prove my worth. Only Jesus can help me believe my to-do list isn't my identity.

I can feel the rhythm within me turning toward restfulness again. I let out a sigh of relief. Today I will not rush. I will not hurry. I will not run.

Today I will walk with God.

And however far we go, it will be enough.

Today

I will not rush.

I will not hurry.

I will not run.

Today I will *walk* with GOD.

—HOLLEY GERTH

You Are a
Child of God

See what great love the Father has given us that we
should be called God's children— and we are!

1 JOHN 3:1

*God, it can feel as if we have to carry the weight
of the world on our shoulders. But the truth is,
we are children who are cared for by a loving Father.
The weight of the world isn't on our shoulders,
it's in Your hands, and we are too. Help us to be
children who rest and trust and delight in You.
Amen.*

You belong to the God who spoke the world into being. You are invited to join in the divine purposes of the kingdom of God, to be a partner in His great and glorious work, but you are not responsible for it.

Asking you to take responsibility for this world would be like asking a toddler to take charge of his father's house. No loving parent would expect that from his child. And your heavenly Father doesn't ask it of you. What does He ask? What any parent does: love and obedience.

You are a child, and life is not meant to be so full of burdens that you can't enjoy what your heavenly Father wants to give you. When your arms and heart and life are so full, how can you receive from Him? Let some of it go. Just lay it down.

You're not meant to live feeling so weighed down. Instead you're created to be lifted up by the heavenly Father who cherishes you more than you can even know.

If We Could Have Coffee

You've *got*
What It Takes

God is able to make every grace overflow to you,
so that in every way, always having everything
you need, you may excel in every good work.

II CORINTHIANS 9:8

*God, sometimes it seems we won't have enough
for what's needed. But we are connected to You,
the endless supplier, the mighty multiplier, the One who is
never empty. You say we can do all things through You,
but You never say we have to do it all. Give us wisdom
to know what is truly ours to do and grant us everything
we need to complete Your will, no more and no less.
Amen.*

Will I have what it takes?

We've all wondered that at some point, haven't we?

When we get the opportunity we really wanted.

When we hear the news we never saw coming.

When life suddenly throws a challenge our way.

On our best and hardest days this is something we all long to know—even if we never put it into words.

One day as I asked "Will I have what it takes?" it seemed God whispered to my scared-silly soul: "What matters isn't if you will have what it takes. What matters is if you will have what needs to be given. And you will. Because I will provide it."

In that moment the pressure lifted from shoulders. I wasn't required to be perfect. I didn't have to make everyone happy. I didn't need to turn into superwoman to accomplish God's purpose for my life. I just needed to believe and receive.

God would give me the strength. He would love others through me. He would do it.

No matter what we're facing, the same is true for all of us. When fear comes, we can pause and say, "Yes, I have what it takes, because I belong to the God who gives all I need...and more."

You Are
Cheered For

What shall we say about
such wonderful things as these? If God is for us,
who can ever be against us?

ROMANS 8:31 NLT

God, You are for us and not against us. You are our
greatest supporter, our most loyal encourager,
the One who never gives up on us. Sometimes it's
so hard to receive that truth because we don't
deserve it and we can't earn it. Help us to remember
that grace is not about us being good enough,
but about You being good to us beyond measure.
Thank You for loving us so well.
Amen.

I stand at the end of a half-marathon waiting for my daughter to come into view. The owner of a local running gear store stands right at the finish line too. He has trained many of these runners.

It makes me teary-eyed when I realize he cheers just as loudly for those who are struggling, exhausted, and out of breath as he does for those who stand tall and sprint strong. He never says, "You're not doing good enough," or shouts, "Get it together!" Instead he just keeps encouraging, keeps affirming, keeps being *for* every single runner. It makes me think of what it might be like when we cross the finish line of this life, when we see Jesus waiting for us at last, when we hear Him say, "Well done, good and faithful servant!" I sometimes picture Him with a look of disappointment or disapproval, but He is our advocate and our coach. He has been in our shoes on this earth. He knows how hard it can be.

We will make it. We will finish our race. We will see His face. We will hear His words up close. Then we will celebrate the victory together—forever.

*W*elcome this

DAY

with

courage.

—HOLLEY
GERTH

You Are in
God's Thoughts

How precious are your thoughts
about me, O God.
They cannot be numbered!

PSALM 139:17 NLT

*God, it's amazing that You are the Creator
and King of everything, yet You care about
the details of our lives. When we're tempted
to think we are alone or on our own,
remind us You are always for us, always working
on our behalf, always thinking of us.
Amen.*

You serve a God who has the hairs on your head not only numbered but memorized. He knows the details of your life even better than you do. He never loses touch with your heart. And because of that, you can always have hope. Because even if you can't see what God is doing, you can trust He is already acting on your behalf. Nothing is too difficult for Him. No challenge is too big. No detail is too small.

The God who spoke the world into being, who holds the stars in place, who sent His Son because He loved you so much is thinking of you. Right now. In this moment. In every moment.

Pause for a moment and let that reality take hold of your heart. You are not alone. You are not overlooked. You are not forgotten.

You never have been.

You never will be.

You are always on God's mind.

And He is always on your side.

What Your Heart Needs for the Hard Days

Your *Worth*

Is Beyond Measure

So don't be afraid;
you are worth more than many sparrows.

MATTHEW 10:31

God, You value each one of us the same.
We matter not because of how much money we have,
how many people know our name,
how many years of education we've completed,
but because You are our Maker. Whatever seems big
in the eyes of this world is still small to You,
and whatever is small in our lives is still big to You
because You love us. Help us to rest
in the truth that we have nothing to prove.
Amen.

The laundry is still unfolded, the emails unanswered, the to-do list undone. I sigh and ask, "Have I been productive at all today?"

Anxiety and accusations are the only response. So I pray, "God, what lie am I believing? And what's the truth that replaces it?" This is a new habit I'm practicing.

It's uncomfortable and hard. Yet in that quiet moment it seems my heart hears a reassuring whisper...

Life isn't about being productive. It's about being purposeful.

I've often believed the lie that God's first priority is what I can produce. But I'm learning that just because something doesn't have tangible results, it doesn't mean it doesn't have eternal impact.

I'm no longer going to ask myself, "Have I been productive today?" Instead I'm going to ask, "Have I been purposeful?" To me that simply means living in love. Sometimes love looks like laundry and answering email and checking off what's on my list. Those are good and worthy things. But often it looks like the exact opposite, like we've done "nothing" at all. And that's okay too.

Our work doesn't determine our worth. Our accomplishments don't earn us God's acceptance. Our value isn't validated by our hustle. We are already and always loved.

Whew. I needed to remember that today. You too?

You Don't Have to Be

Perfect

for God to Use You

Because of the LORD's faithful love we do not
perish, for His mercies never end. They are new
every morning; great is Your faithfulness!

LAMENTATIONS 3:22–23

*God, I know I'm not perfect. But I believe
You can use me anyway. I offer myself
to You just as I am today. I will again tomorrow.
No matter what mistakes I make.
No matter how many times I fall down.
I will get back up and serve You forever.*

Amen.

God has this funny tendency. He chooses messy, broken people to do extraordinary, God-glorifying things. An adulterer to lead His holy nation (David). A prostitute in the lineage of the Messiah (Rahab). An accomplice of murder to spread the gospel (Paul). Even Peter, one of the disciples, denied Jesus three times on the night before He went to the cross.

I don't know how to explain this part of how God works. It's so different than how we as humans would do it. We would choose the most perfect among us, the steadiest, the least risky. But God scandalously and stubbornly chooses sinners instead.

Are you feeling unworthy today? Do you wonder how God could even want you when He knows everything about you? Push aside those lies and doubts, the fears and failures, and take hold again of the One who will never let you go. Then welcome this day with courage, faith, and the belief that nothing you do (or don't do) can overcome His love for you.

Opening the Door to Your God-Sized Dream

Your *Story* Isn't Over

Many are the plans in a person's heart,
but it is the LORD's purpose that prevails.

PROVERBS 19:21 NIV

God, You are the Author of our lives.
You are the One who speaks truth to our hearts.
When the lies get loud, we choose to listen to You.
Tell us who we are, remind us of what's true.
Help us to tell each other too. We want
our lives to be stories that bring You glory.
Amen.

We are living a story today. A story crafted and told by the Author of heaven. The star-scatterer. The mountain-mover. The water-walker.

In the day-to-day, it doesn't feel like a story. It feels like dishes in the sink. Reports on the desk. Another mile behind the steering wheel of the car. There is so much we do not know, that we will not know, but we can be certain of this: the Author is good and we are loved.

There is a God at work who has always been speaking, always been creating beauty out of the broken. "Jesus also did many other things. If they were all written down, I suppose the whole world could not contain the books that would be written" (John 21:25 NLT). Jesus is still doing many other things. He is not done with history. He is not finished with the part of it that is our story either. Whatever scene we find ourselves in today, it is not the final page. Hold on, there is a turning coming. There is more than this, more than here and now. We have not yet seen the there and then.

We are overcomers. We are warriors. We are a force to be reckoned with in this world. And whatever the future brings, our God is still holding the pen. He is the only One who gets to write "The End."

Strong, Brave, Loved

ACKNOWLEDGMENTS

I'm grateful to the DaySpring team for the opportunity to do this book together! Thank you to Gini Wietecha and Lisa Stilwell for being excellent editors. And thank you to Heather Steck for her beautiful design work. Special thanks to Revell, a division of Baker Publishing Group, for permission to include content from Holley Gerth's books in What's True About You. *To find all of Holley's books, visit your favorite book retailer or holleygerth.com.*

ENDNOTES

Grateful acknowledgment *is given to Baker Book/Revell Publishers for permission to reprint the copyrighted material. All copyrights are held by Holley Gerth. You can find these titles wherever books are sold.*

You Are Free: Gerth, Holley. *If We Could Have Coffee...* (E-book Shorts): *30 Days of Heart-to-Heart Encouragement.* Michigan: Revell, 2014. Kindle.

You Are Seen: Gerth, Holley. *You're Going to Be Okay: Encouraging Truth Your Heart Needs to Hear, Especially on the Hard Days.* Michigan: Revell, 2014. Kindle.

You Don't Have to Feel Ready: Gerth, Holley. *Strong, Brave, Loved* (E-book Shorts): *21 Ways to a Fierce-Hearted Life.* Michigan: Revell, 2018. Kindle.

You Are Provided for by God: Gerth, Holley. *The Encouragement Project* (E-book Shorts): *21 Heart-to-Heart Ways to Show You Care.* Michigan: Revell, 2015. Kindle.

You Are God's Friend: Gerth, Holley. *Hope Your Heart Needs: 52 Encouraging Reminders of How God Cares for You.* Michigan: Revell, 2018. Kindle.

You Are Victorious: Gerth, Holley. *If We Could Have Coffee...* (E-book Shorts): *30 Days of Heart-to-Heart Encouragement.* Michigan: Revell, 2014. Kindle.

You Are Chosen: Gerth, Holley. *You're Made for a God-Sized Dream: Opening the Door to All God Has for You.* Michigan: Revell, 2013. Kindle.

You Are Beyond Compare: Gerth, Holley. *If We Could Have Coffee...* (E-book Shorts): *30 Days of Heart-to-Heart Encouragement.* Michigan: Revell, 2014. Kindle.

You Are Loved No Matter What: Gerth, Holley. *You're Loved No Matter What: Freeing Your Heart from the Need to Be Perfect.* Michigan: Revell, 2015. Kindle.

Your Brokenness Is Part of Your Beauty: Gerth, Holley. *You're Already Amazing: Embracing Who You Are, Becoming All God Created You to Be.* Michigan: Revell, 2012. Kindle.

You Are Never a Failure: Gerth, Holley. *Opening the Door to Your God-Sized Dream: 40 Days of Encouragement for Your Heart.* Michigan: Revell, 2013. Kindle.

You Really Are Forgiven: Gerth, Holley. *You're Already Amazing: Embracing Who You Are, Becoming All God Created You to Be.* Michigan: Revell, 2012. Kindle.

You Are Called: Gerth, Holley. *You're Made for a God-Sized Dream: Opening the Door to All God Has for You.* Michigan: Revell, 2013. Kindle.

You'll Have the Wisdom You Need: Gerth, Holley. *The Encouragement Project* (E-book Shorts): *21 Heart-to-Heart Ways to Show You Care.* Michigan: Revell, 2015. Kindle.

You Are Accepted: Gerth, Holley. *If We Could Have Coffee...* (E-book Shorts): *30 Days of Heart-to-Heart Encouragement.* Michigan: Revell, 2014. Kindle.

Your Tears Matter to God: Gerth, Holley. *What Your Heart Needs for the Hard Days: 52 Encouraging Truths to Hold On To.* Michigan: Revell, 2014. Kindle.

You Are Going to Be Okay: Gerth, Holley. *You're Going to Be Okay: Encouraging Truth Your Heart Needs to Hear, Especially on the Hard Days.* Michigan: Revell, 2014. Kindle.

You Are in God's Care: Gerth, Holley. *Hope Your Heart Needs: 52 Encouraging Reminders of How God Cares for You.* Michigan: Revell, 2018. Kindle.

You Are Needed: Gerth, Holley. *You're Made for a God-Sized Dream: Opening the Door to All God Has for You.* Michigan: Revell, 2013. Kindle.

You Are a Child of God: Gerth, Holley. *If We Could Have Coffee...* (E-book Shorts): *30 Days of Heart-to-Heart Encouragement.* Michigan: Revell, 2014. Kindle.

You Are in God's Thoughts: Gerth, Holley. *What Your Heart Needs for the Hard Days: 52 Encouraging Truths to Hold On To.* Michigan: Revell, 2014. Kindle.

You Don't Have to Be Perfect for God to Use You: Gerth, Holley. *Opening the Door to Your God-Sized Dream: 40 Days of Encouragement for Your Heart.* Michigan: Revell, 2013. Kindle.

LIVE YOUR FAITH

Dear Friend,

     This book was prayerfully crafted with you, the reader, in mind—every word, every sentence, every page—was thoughtfully written, designed, and packaged to encourage you...right where you are this very moment. At DaySpring, our vision is to see every person experience the life-changing message of God's love. So, as we worked through rough drafts, design changes, edits and details, we prayed for you to deeply experience His unfailing love, indescribable peace, and pure joy. It is our sincere hope that through these Truth-filled pages your heart will be blessed, knowing that God cares about you—your desires and disappointments, your challenges and dreams.

He knows. He cares. He loves you unconditionally.

BLESSINGS!
THE DAYSPRING BOOK TEAM